Catalog of Icon Images Written by

By Ellen Tomaszewski

Catalog of Icon Images
By Ellen Tomaszewski

This catalog contains images of most of the icons written by Ellen Tomaszewski up to this point. Of course, it is by no means an exhaustive list of what is possible. Ellen loves writing icons, and has tried to capture the beauty and the mystery of the saint in each image.

etcetera press

Published by Etcetera Press LLC

© 2017

ISBN: 978-1-936824-59-5

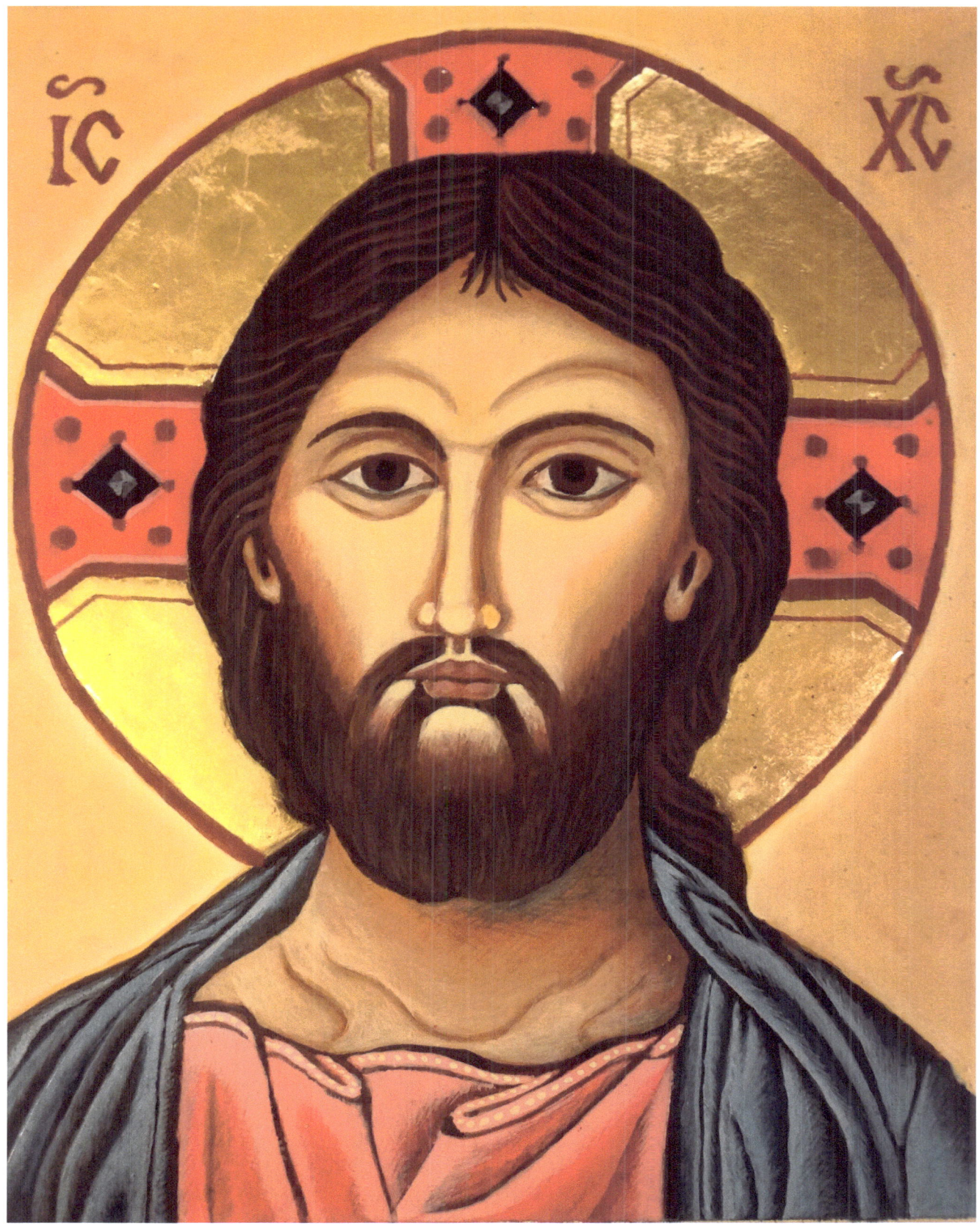

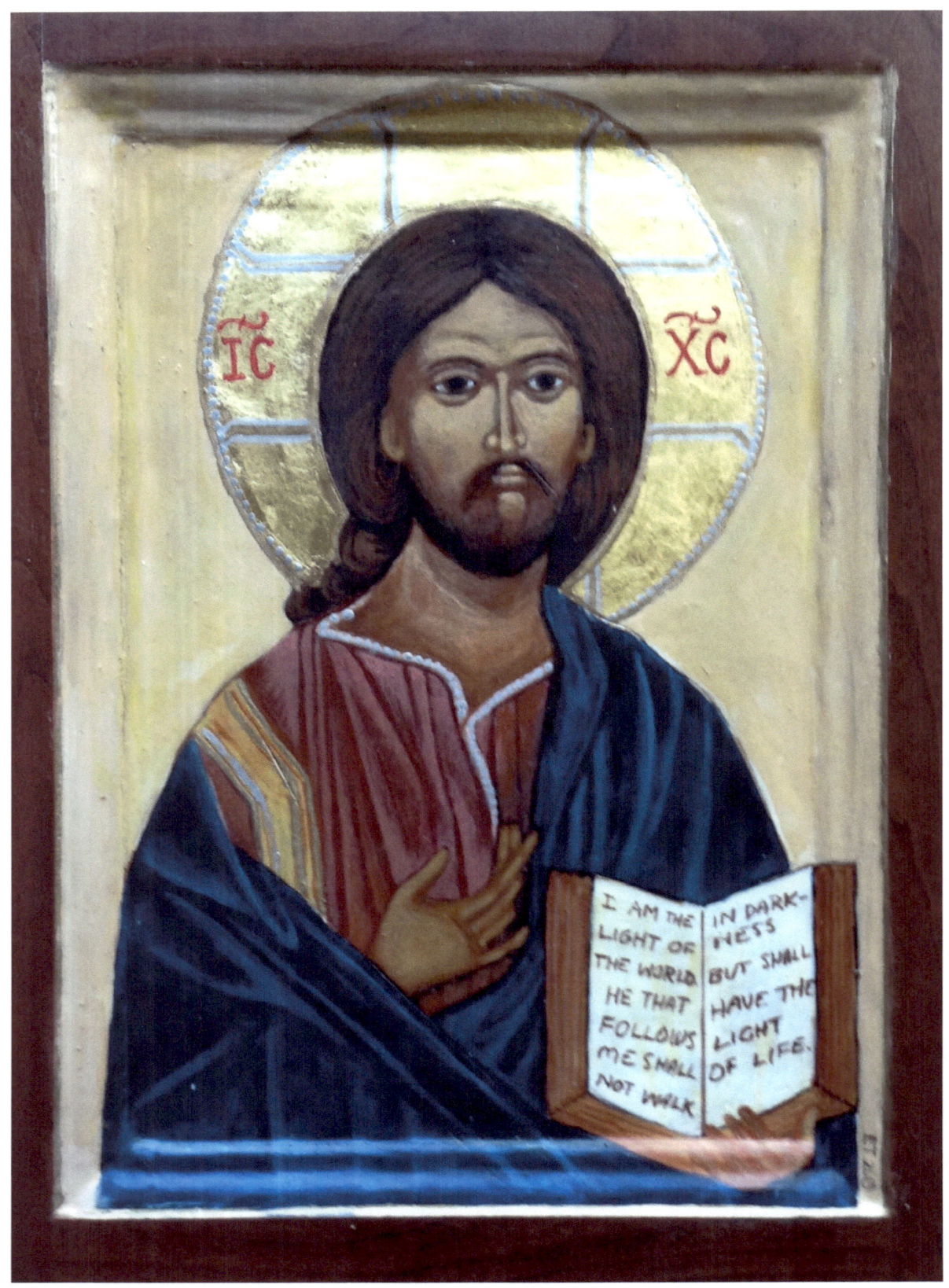

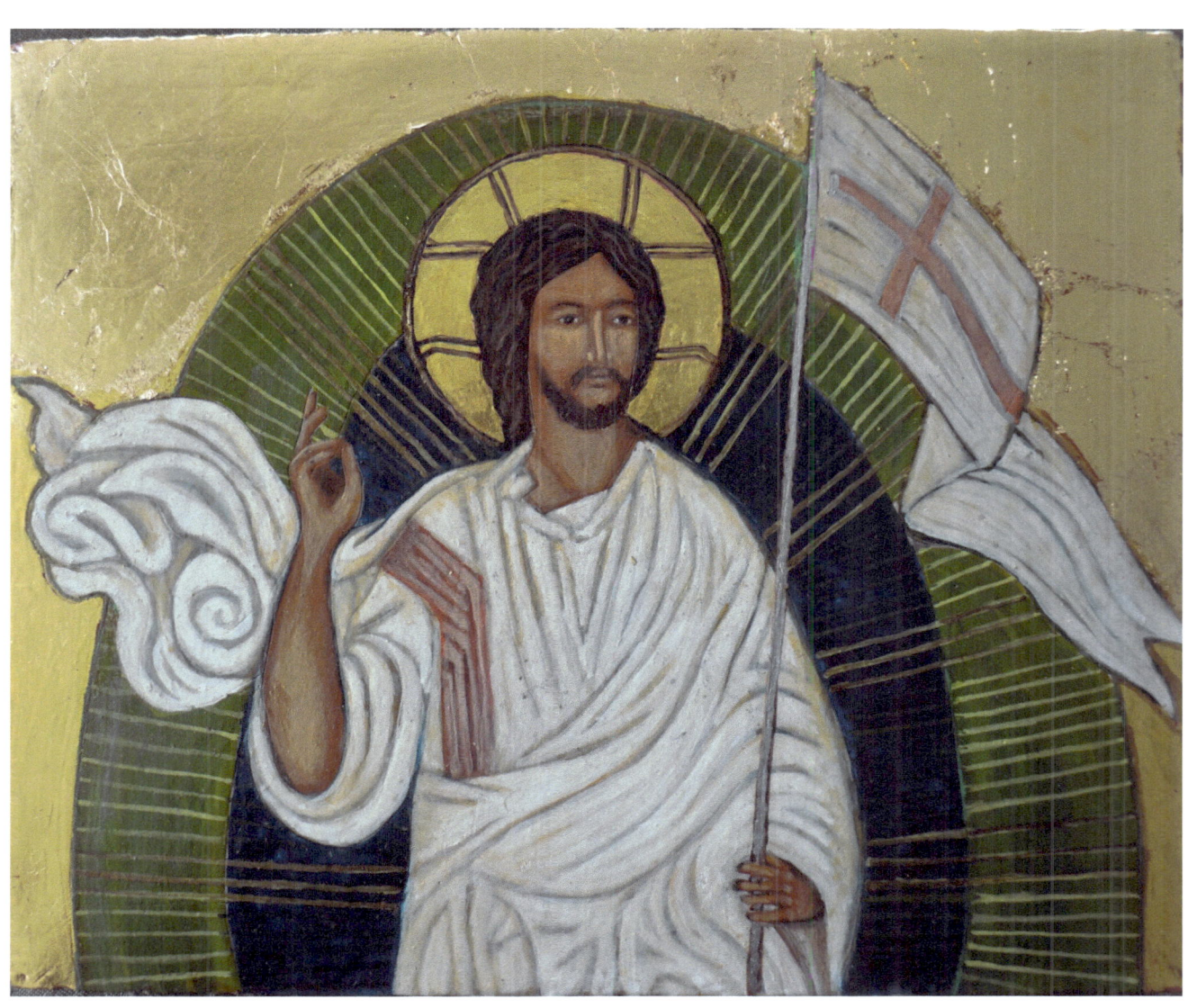

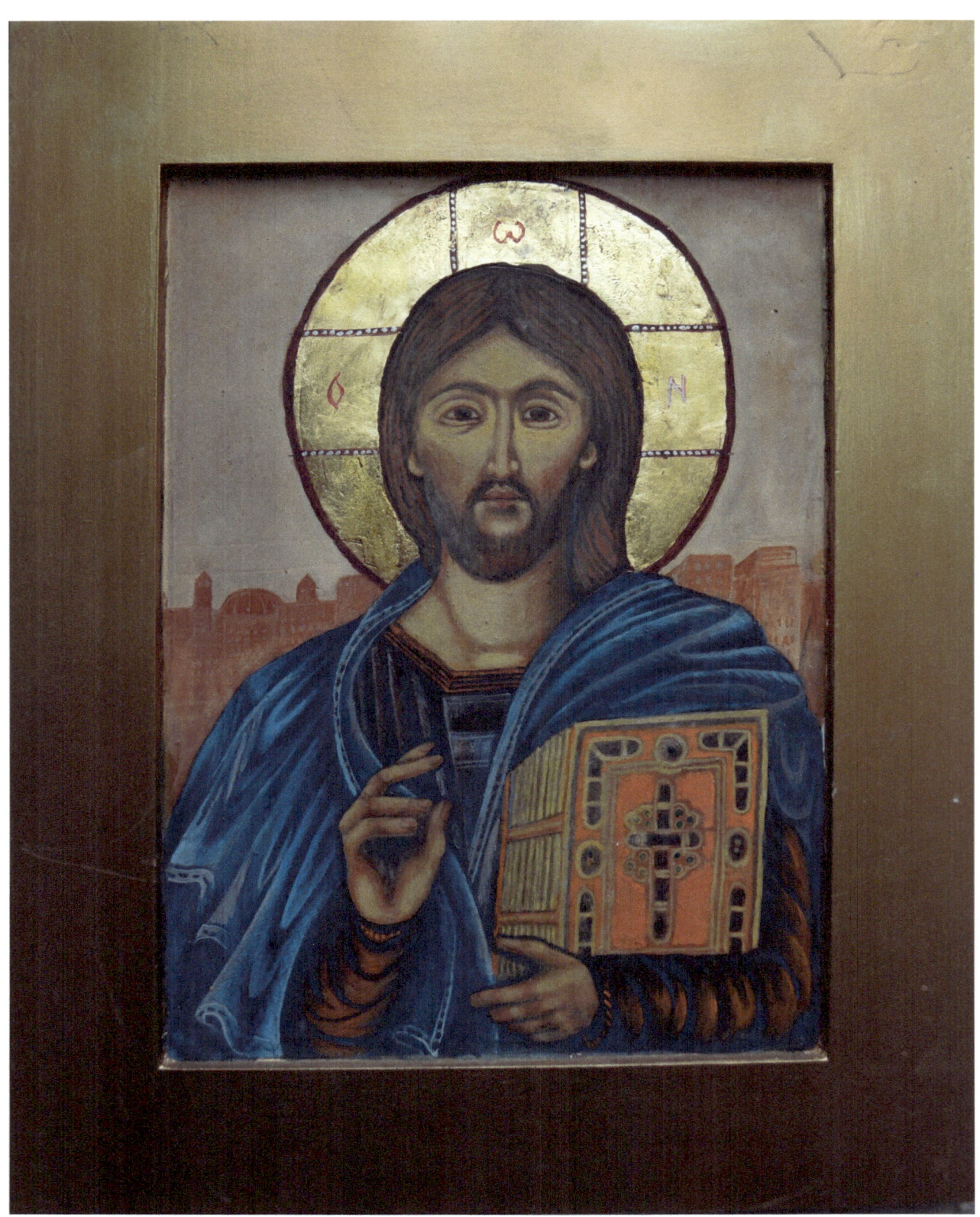

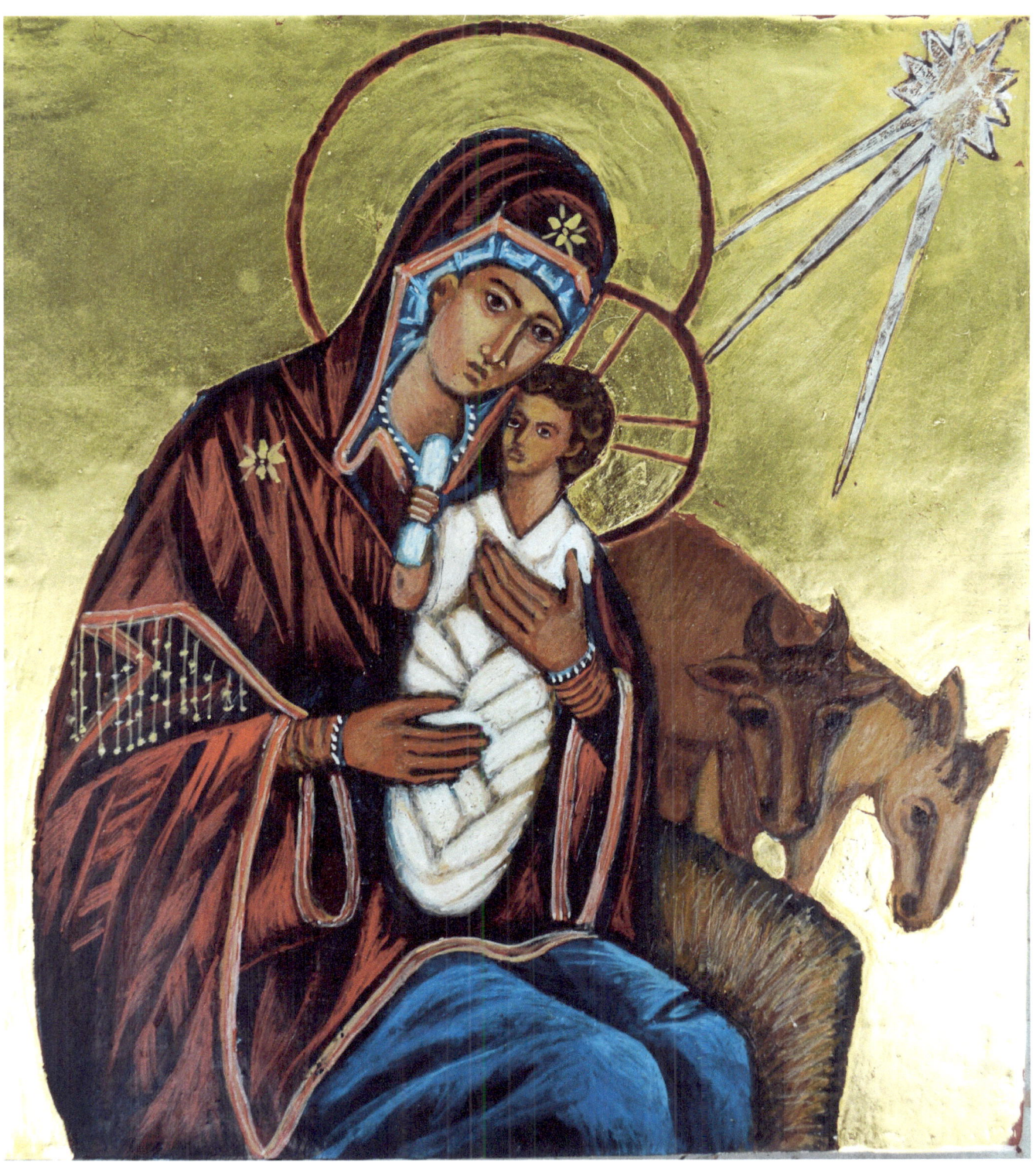

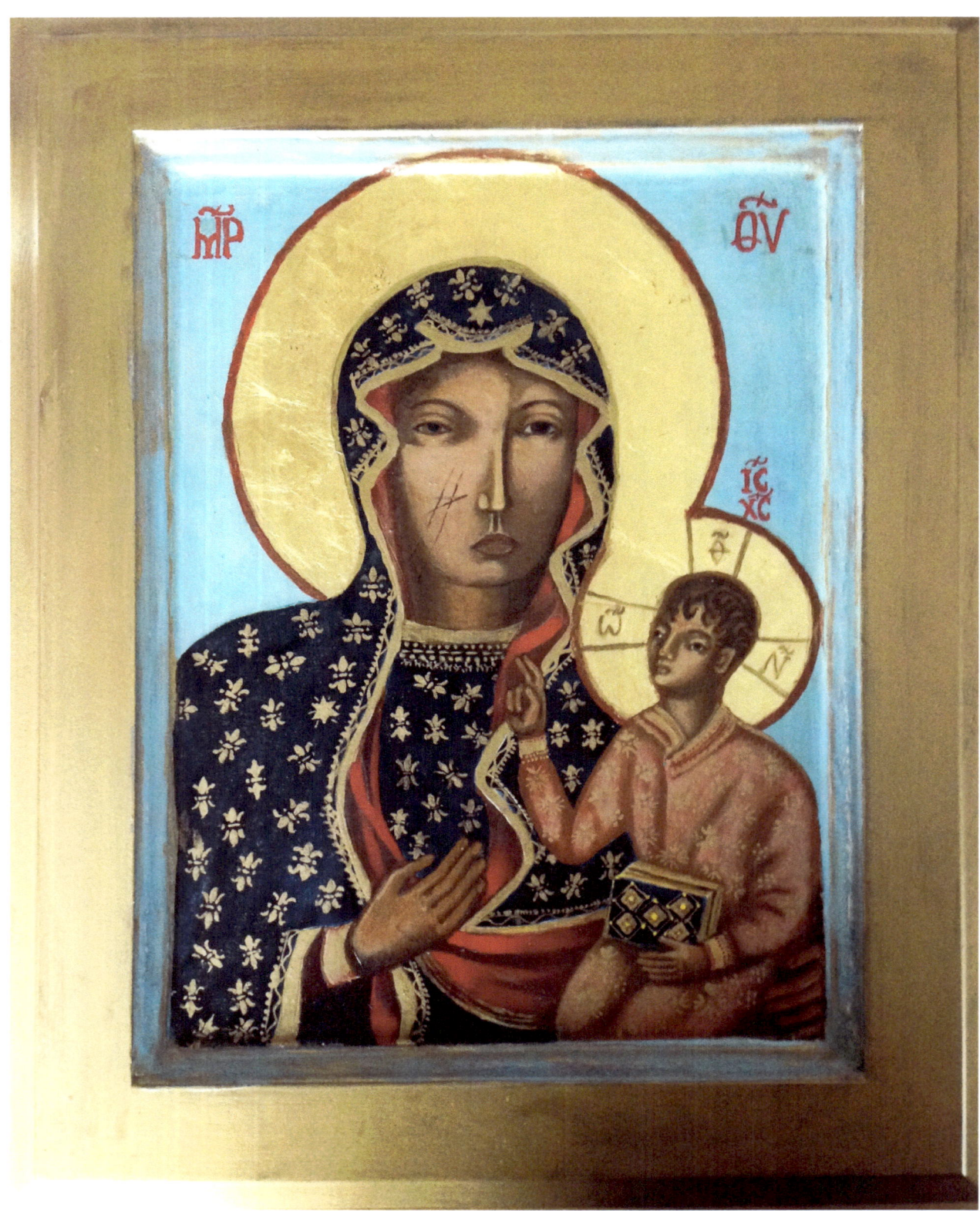

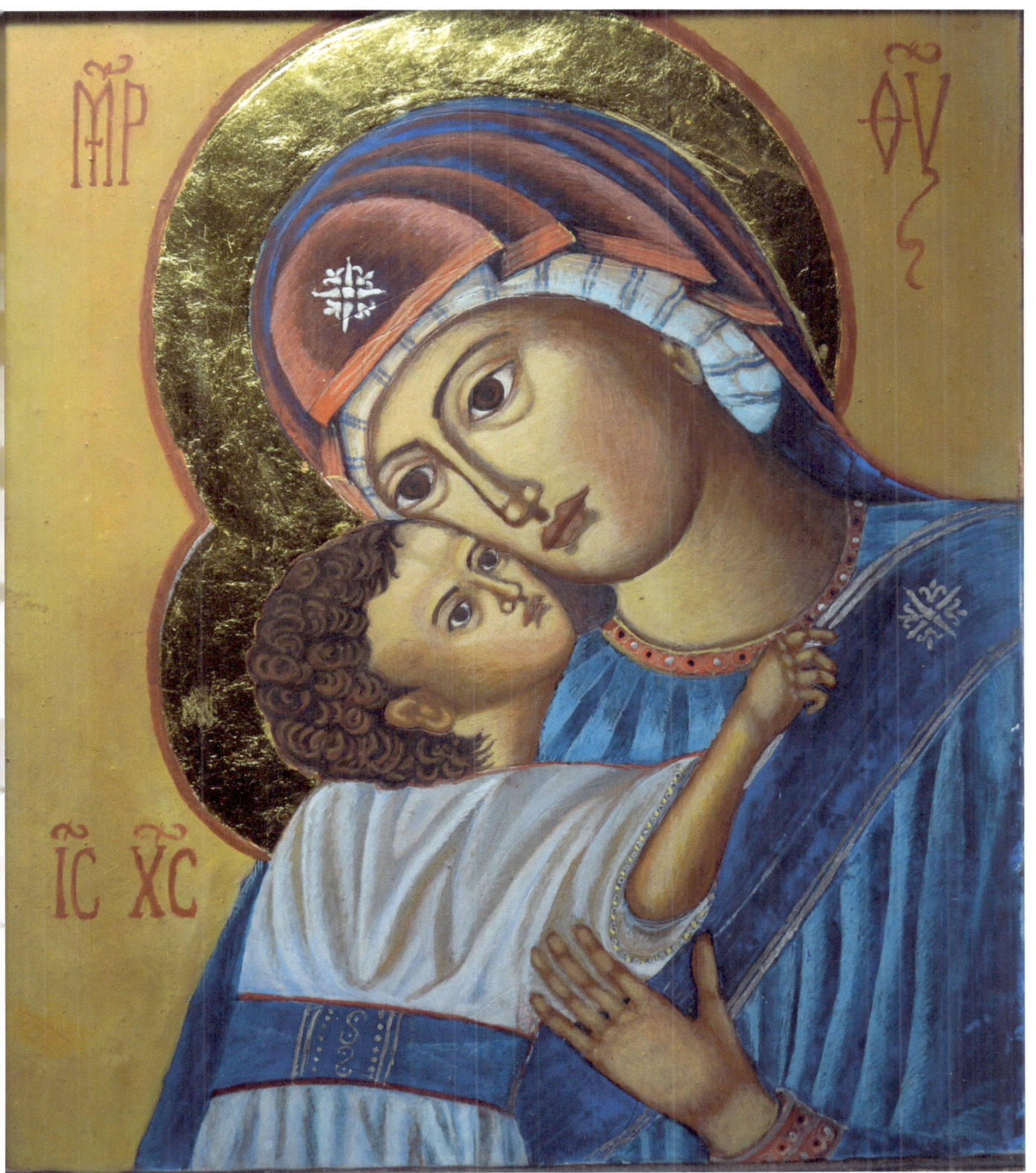

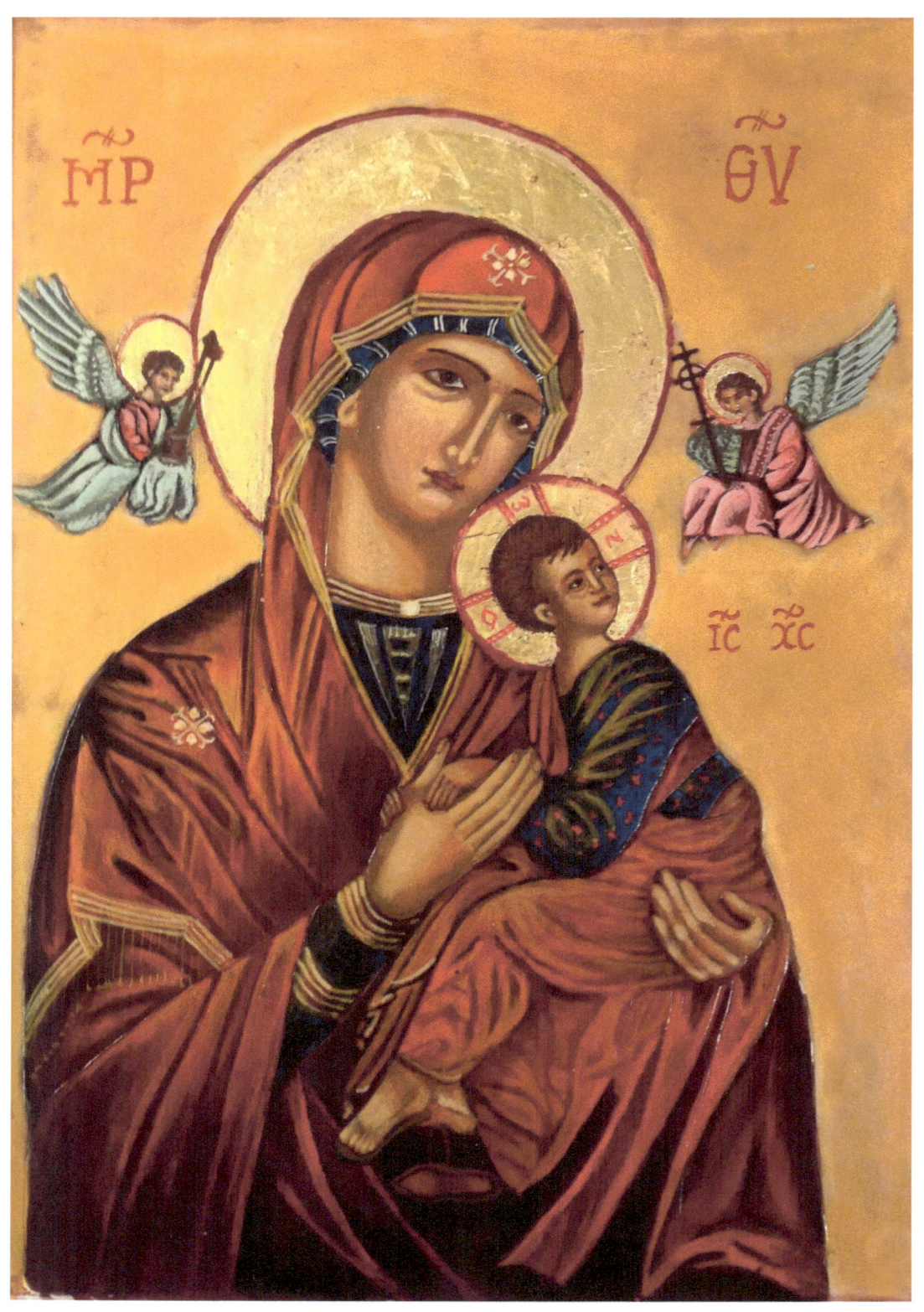

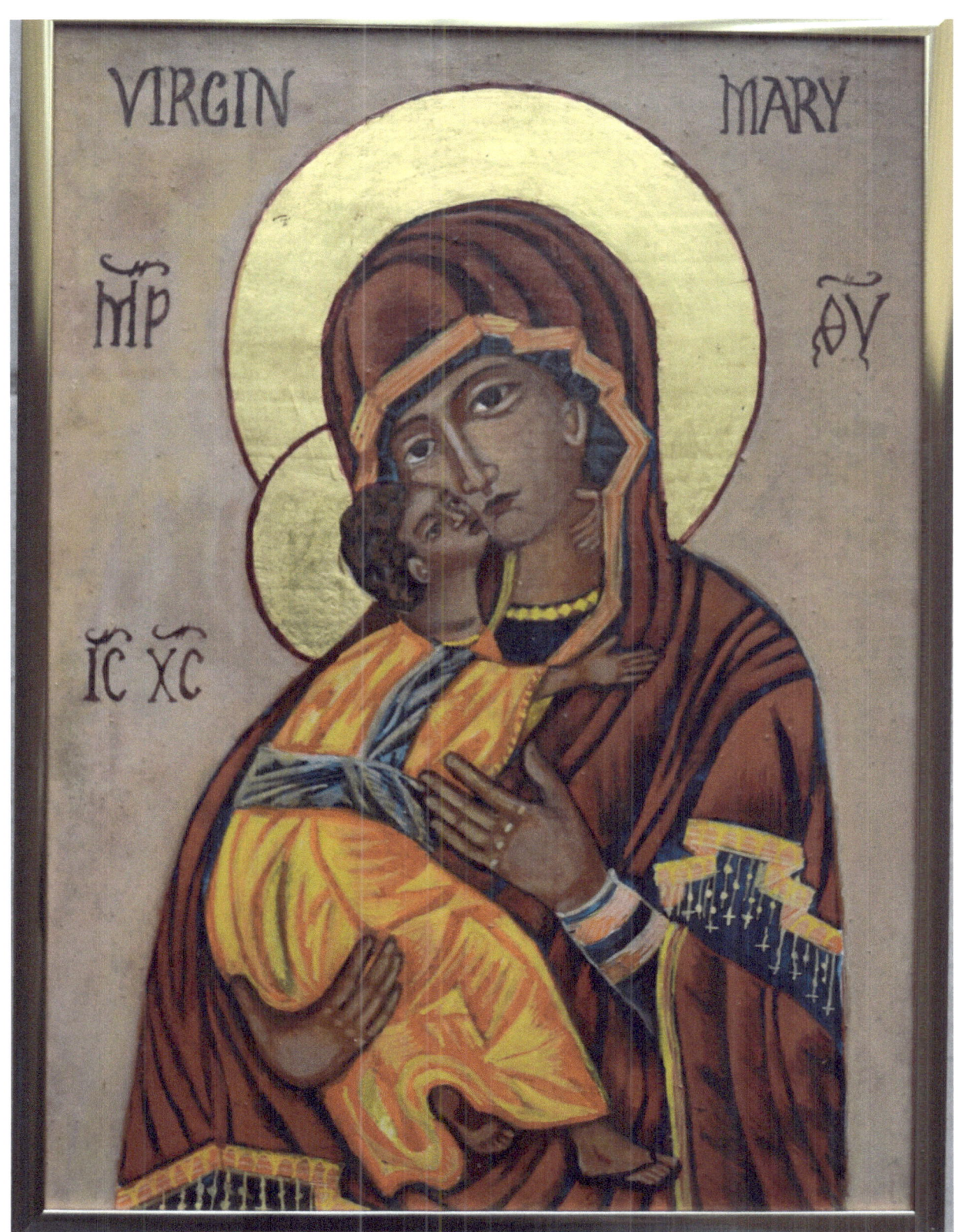

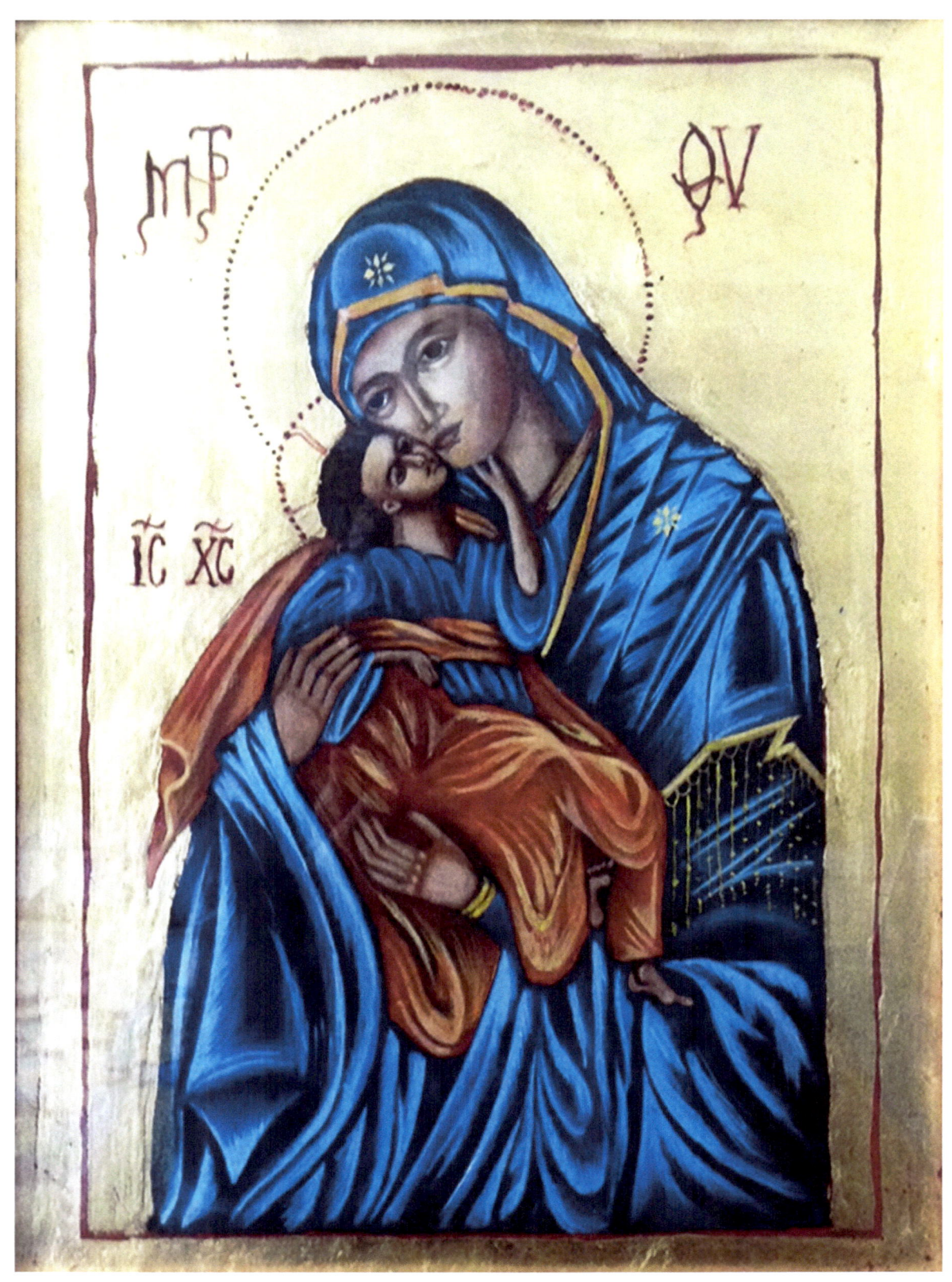

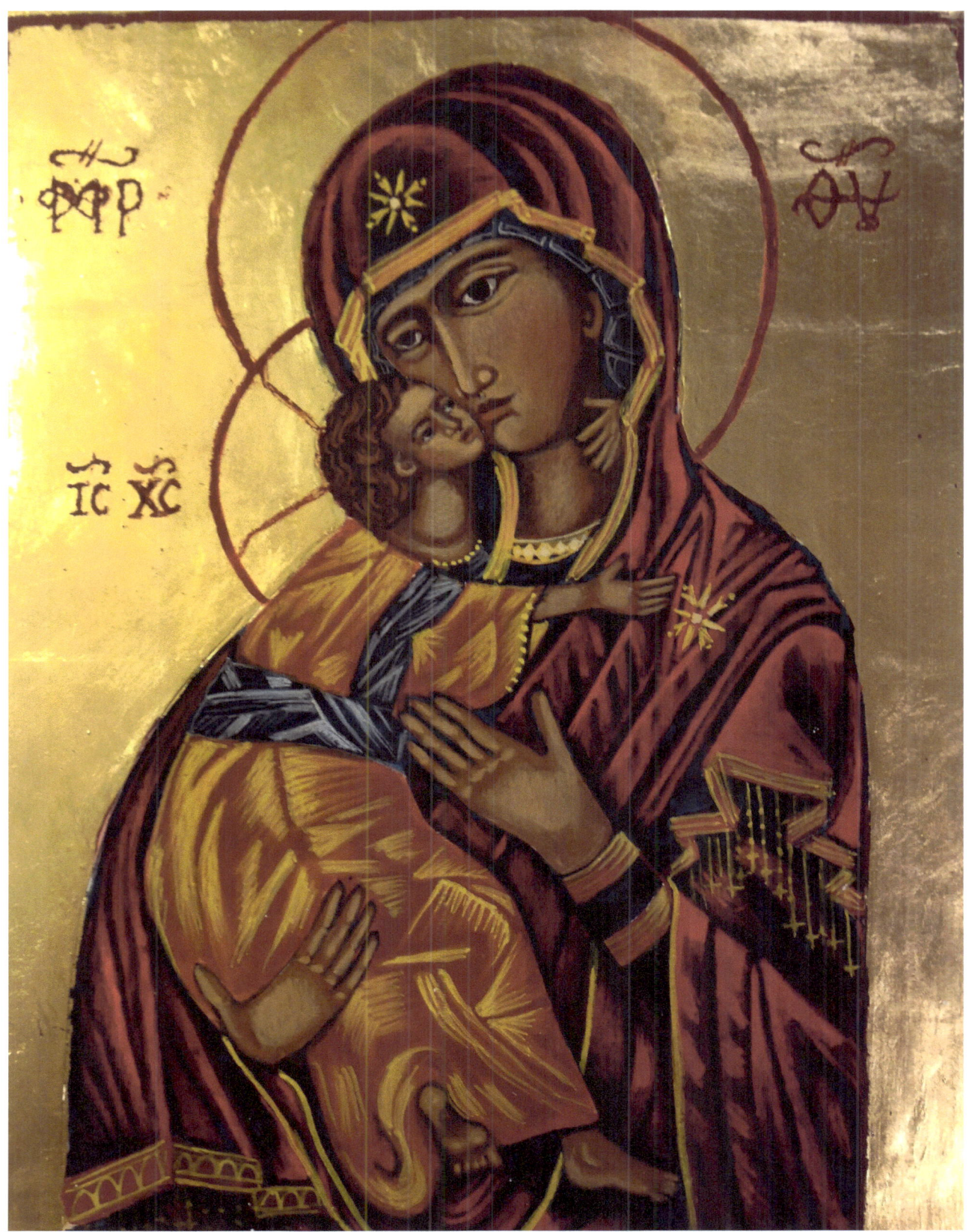

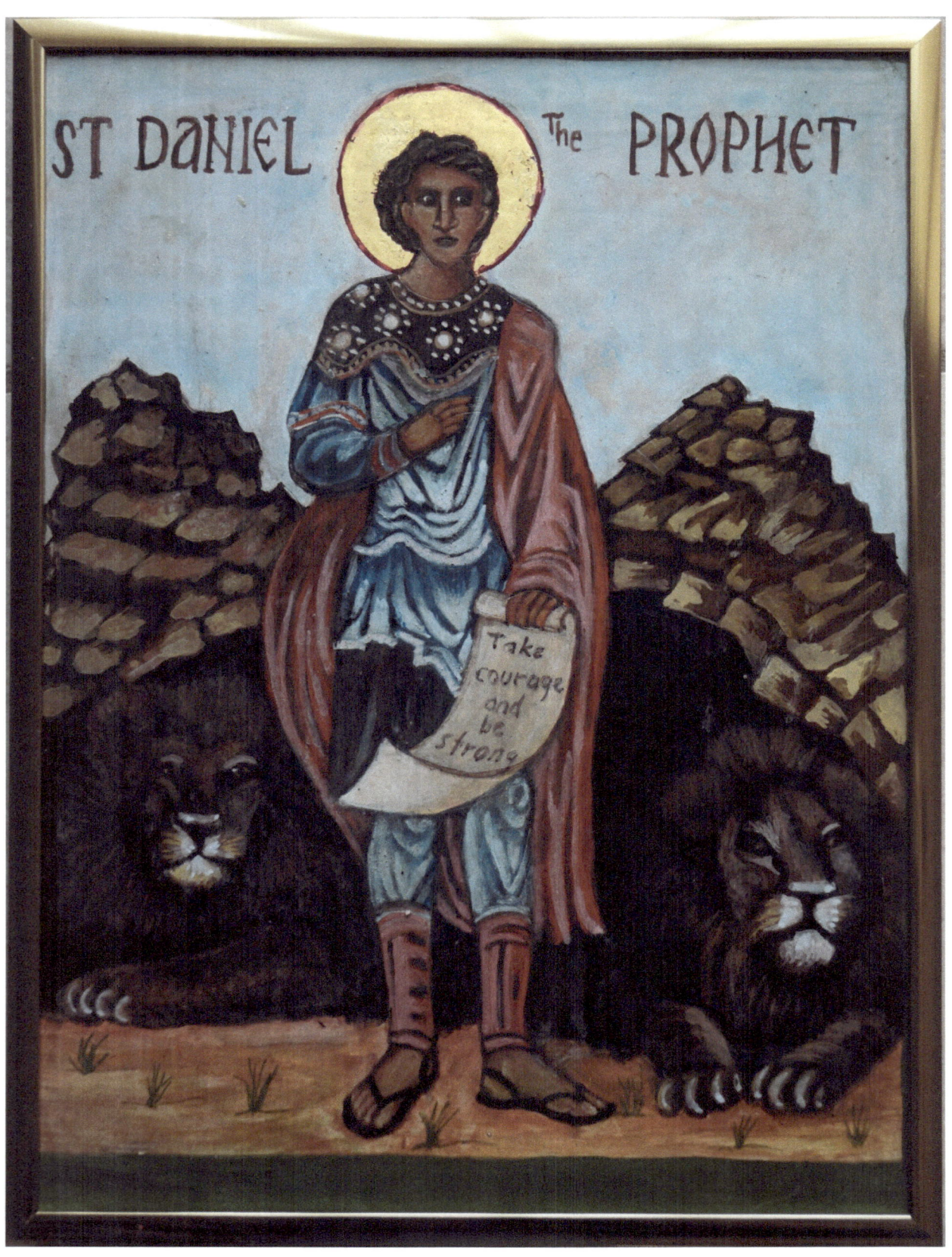

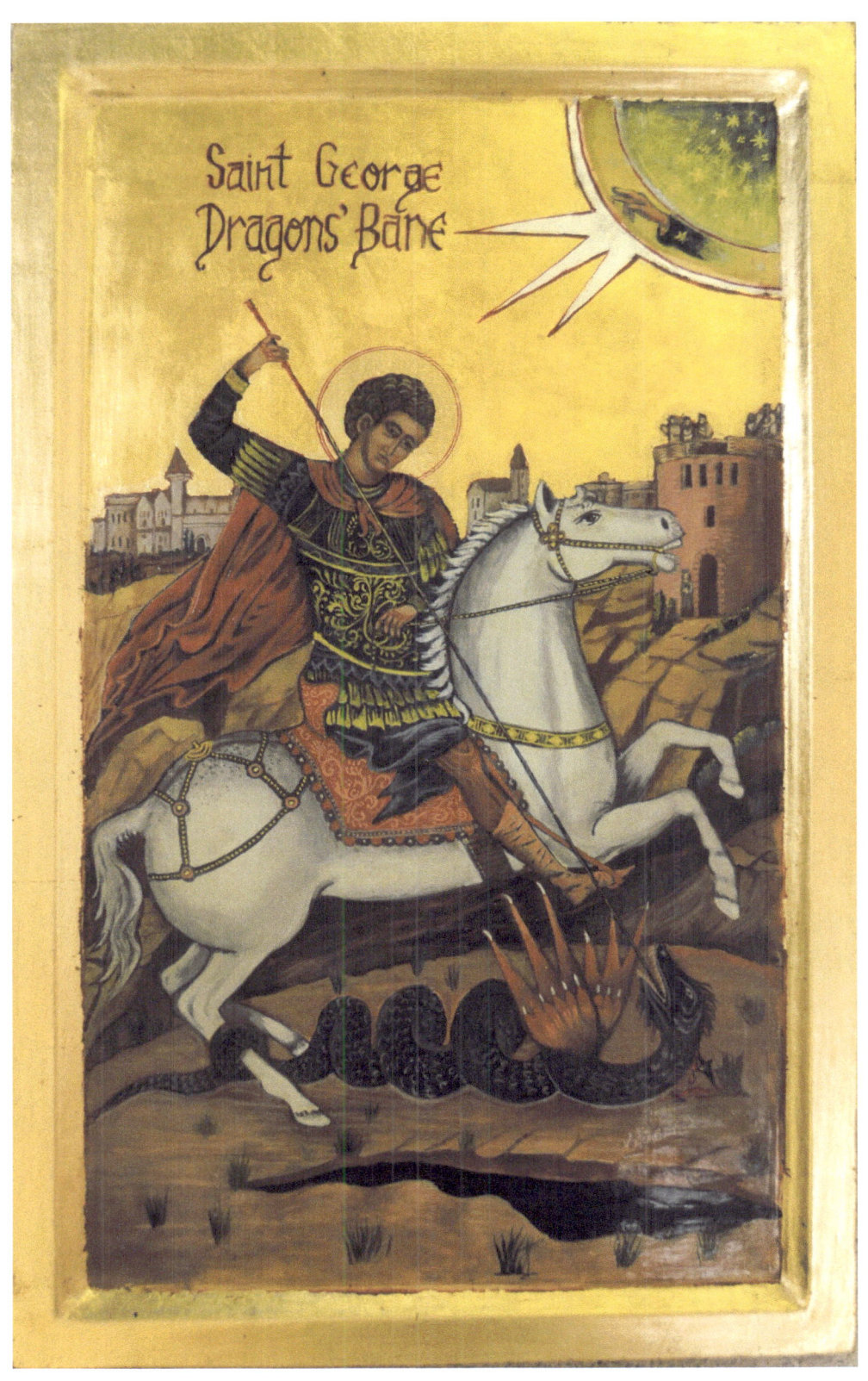

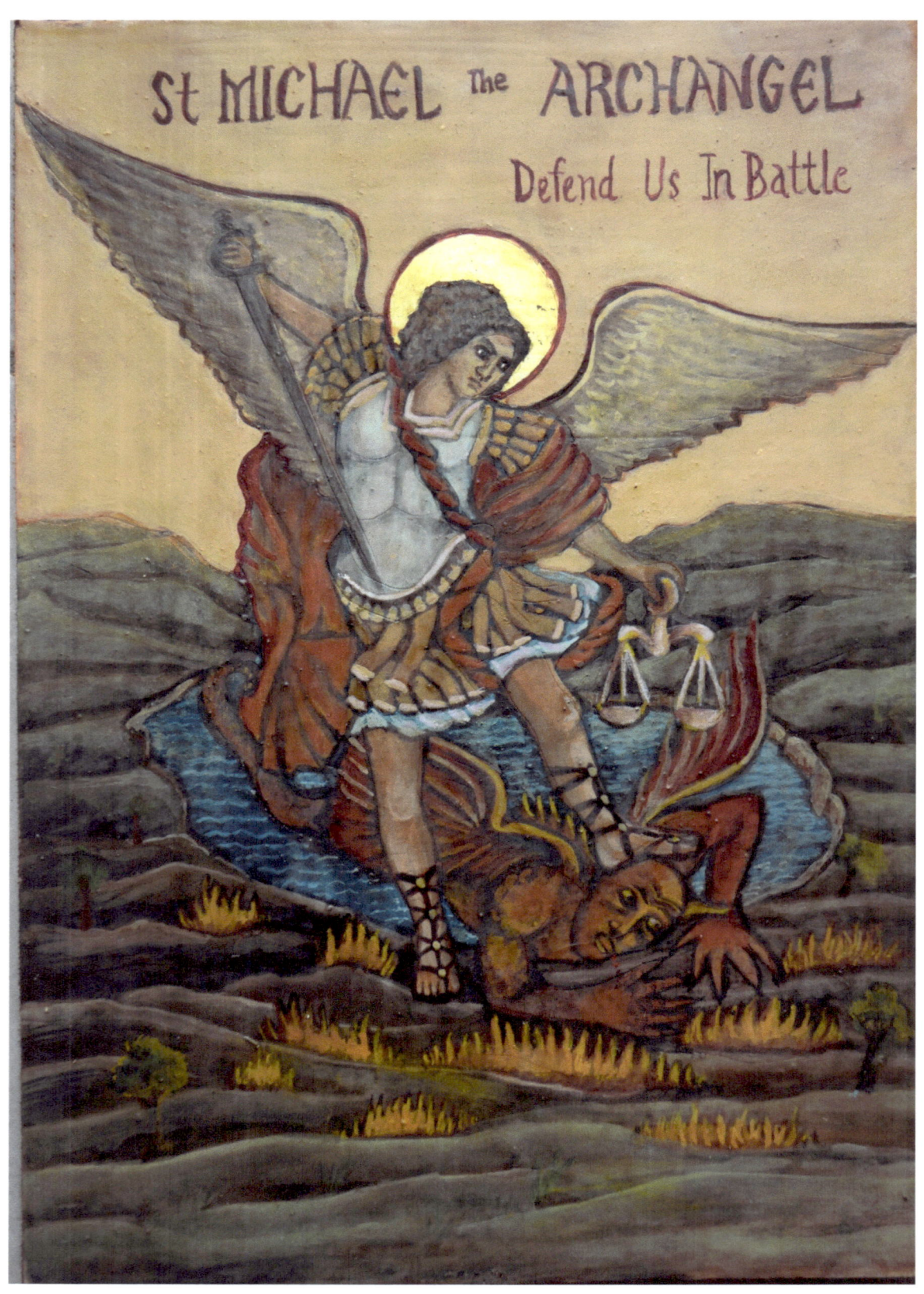

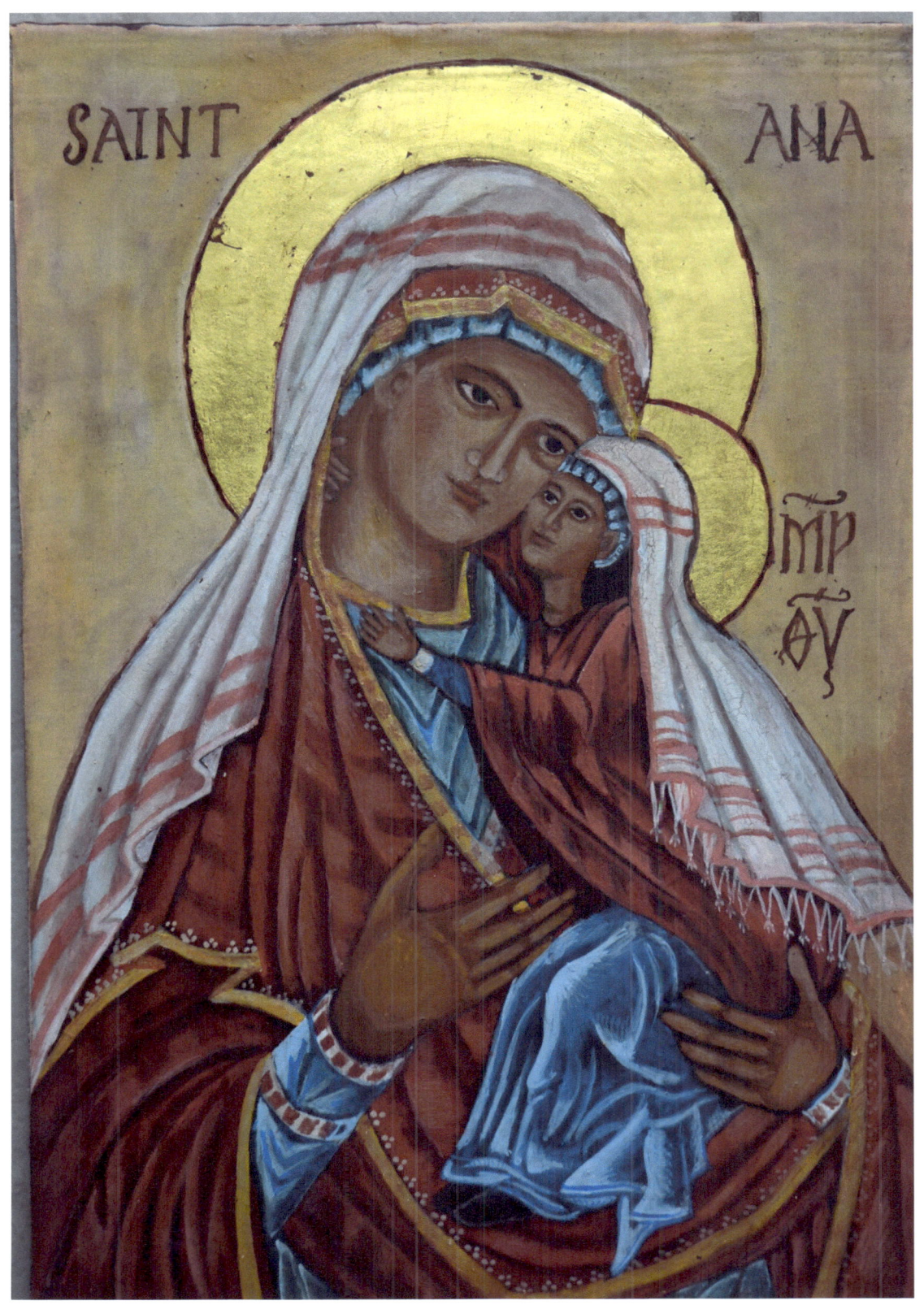

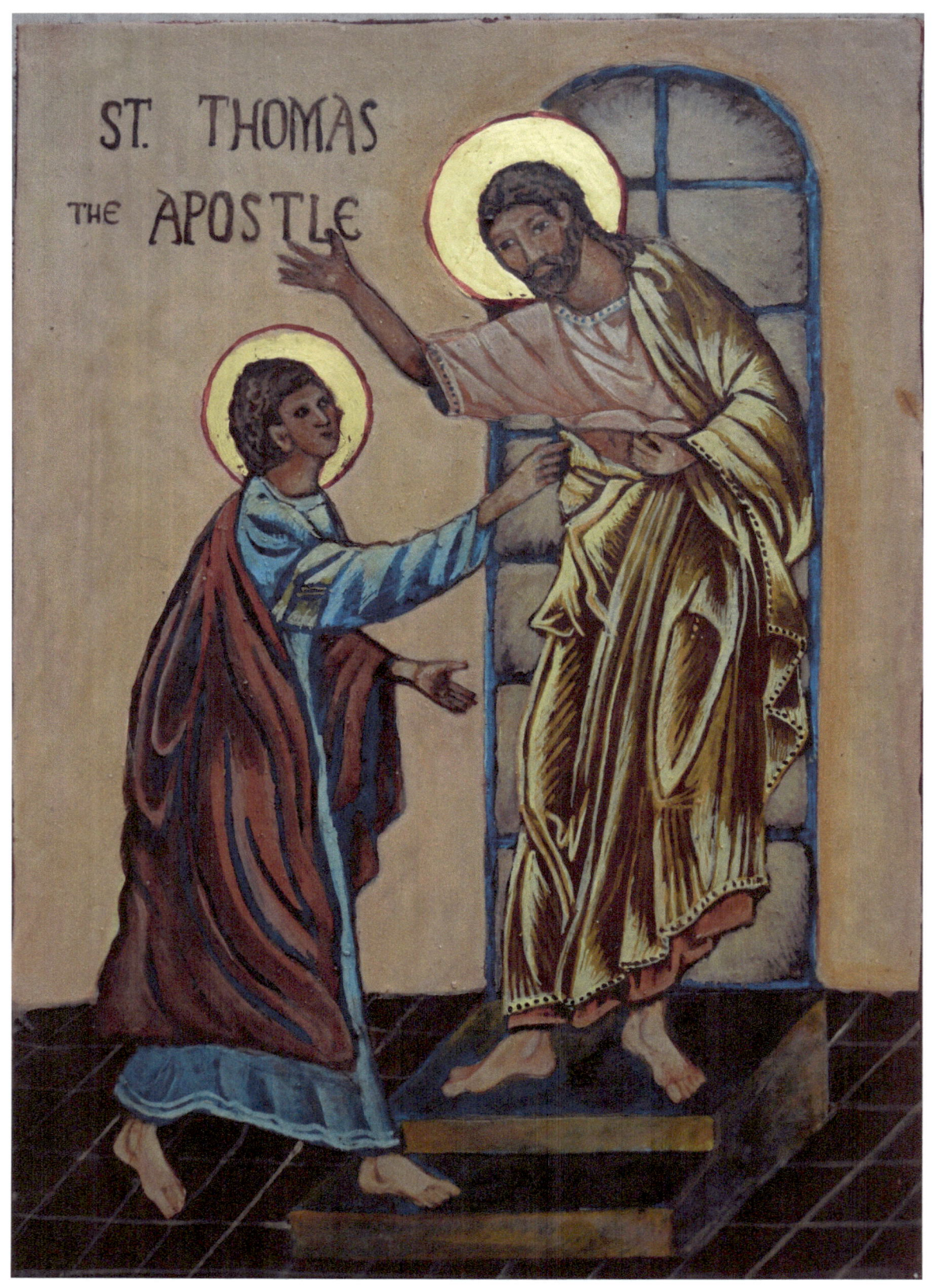

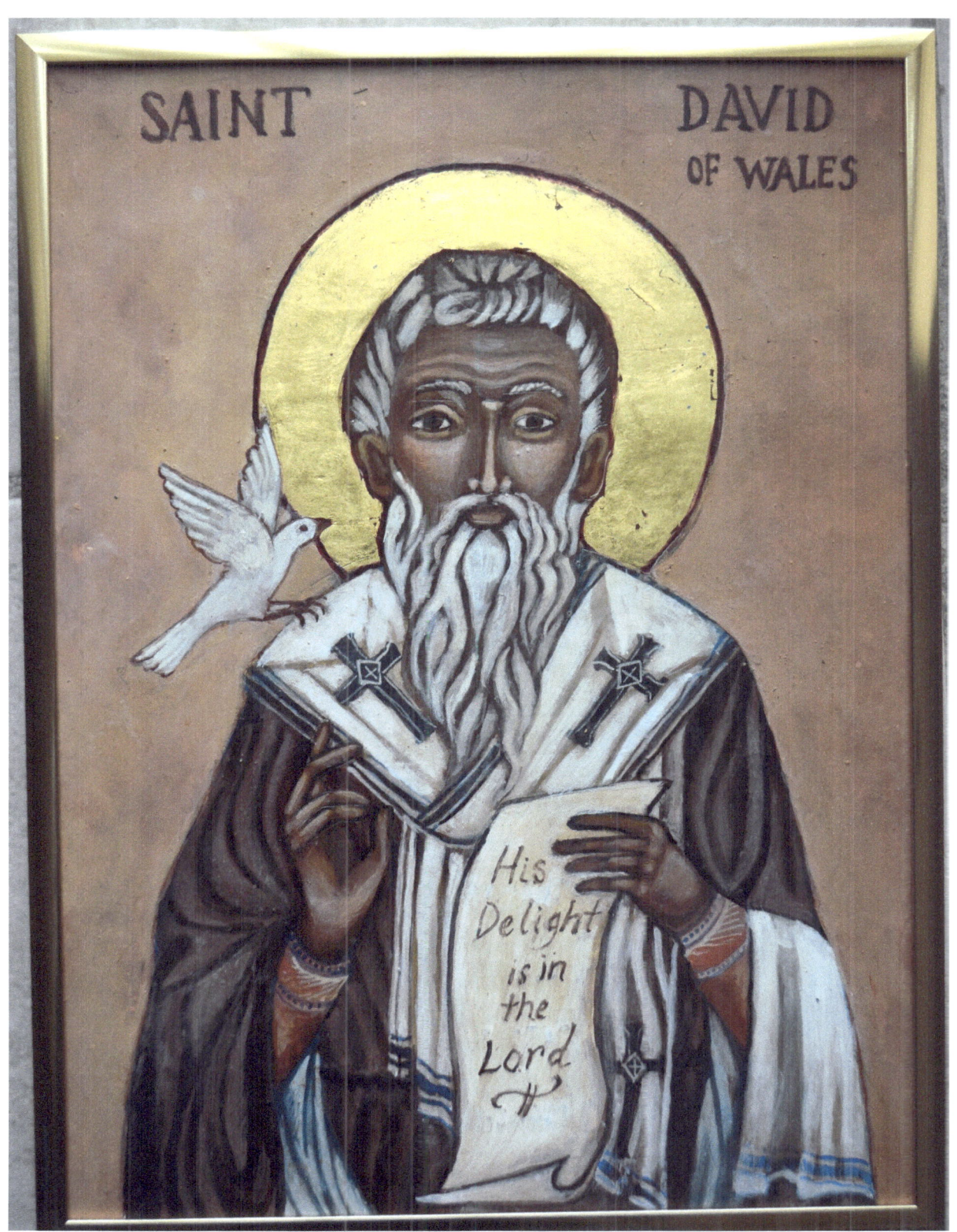

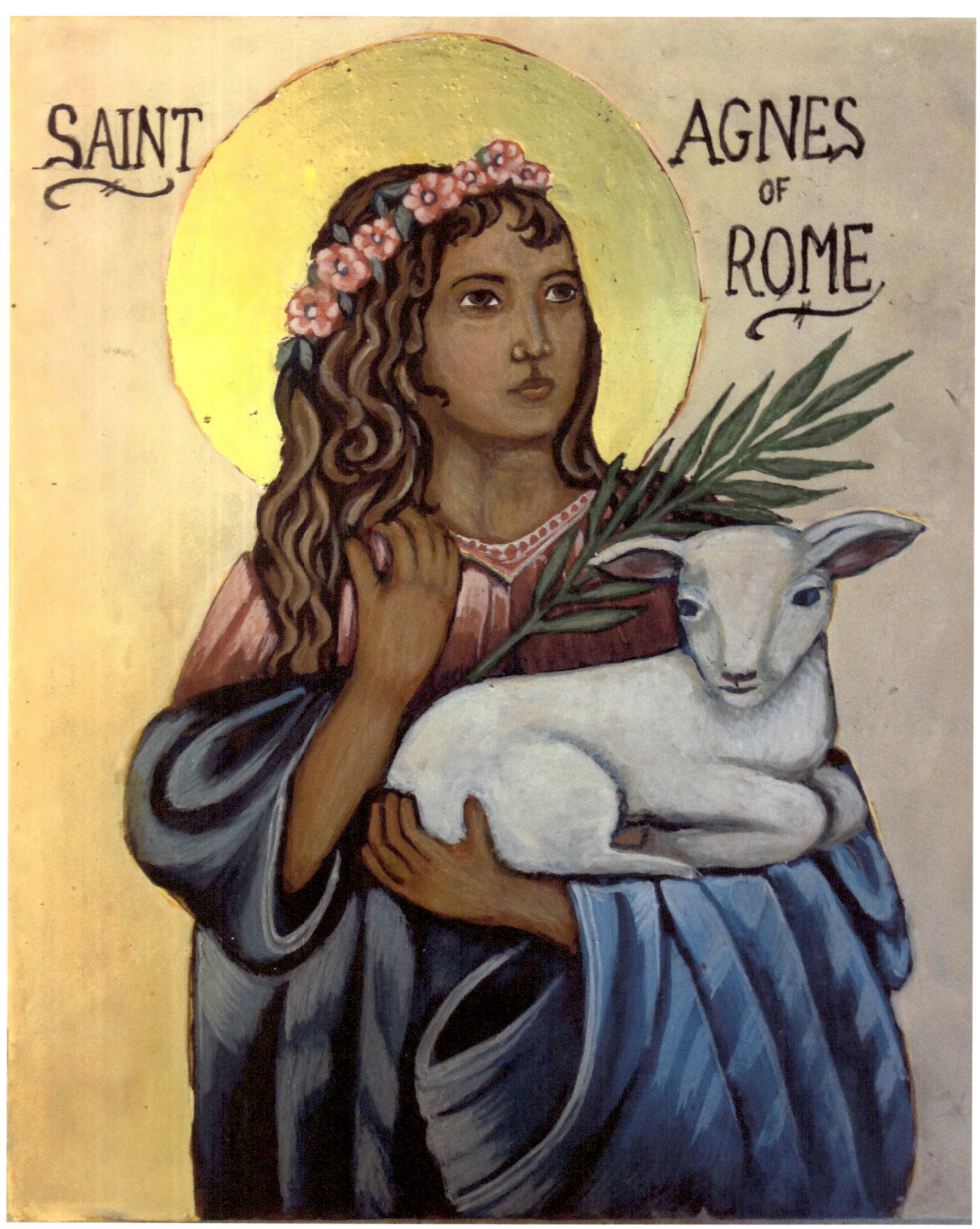

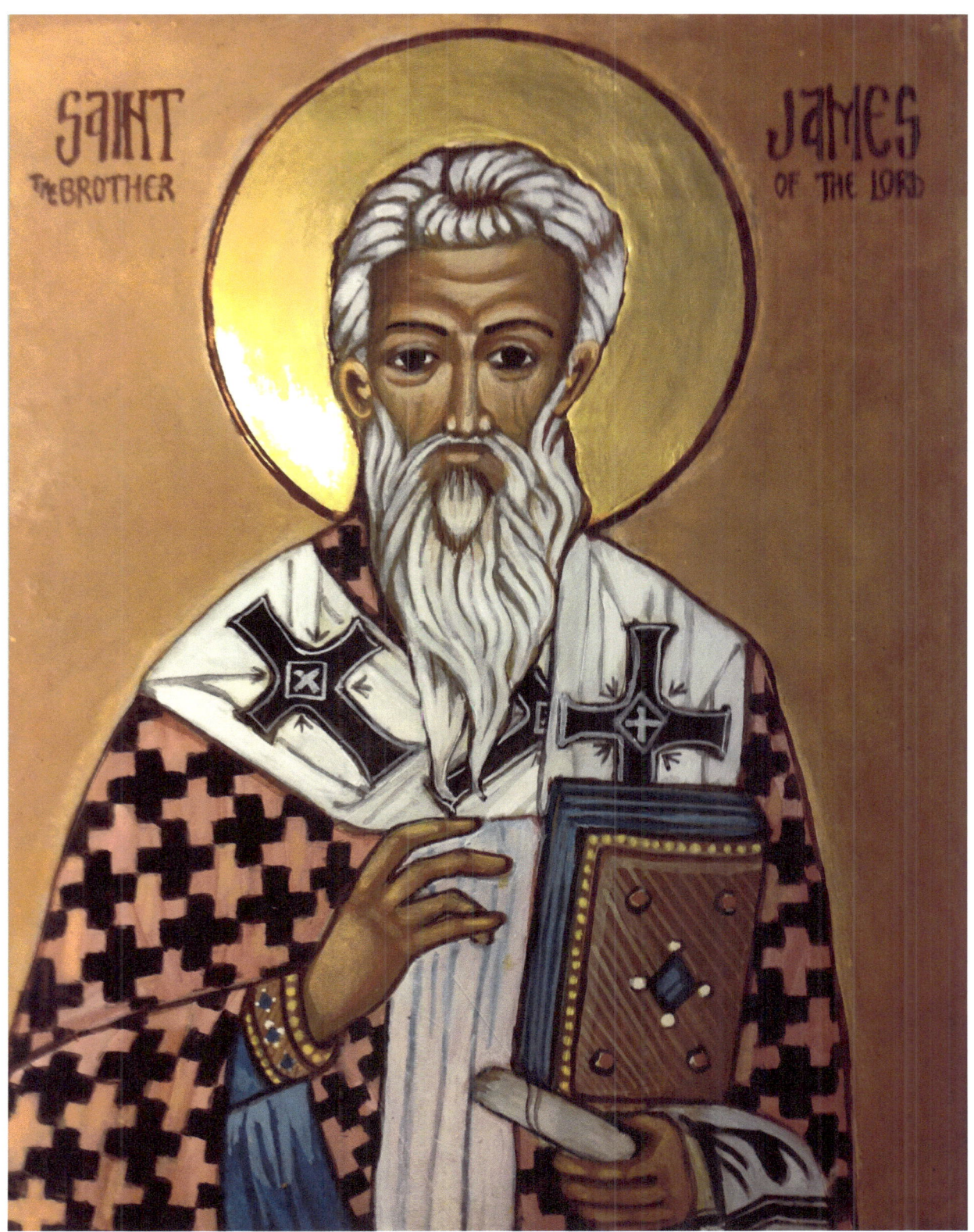

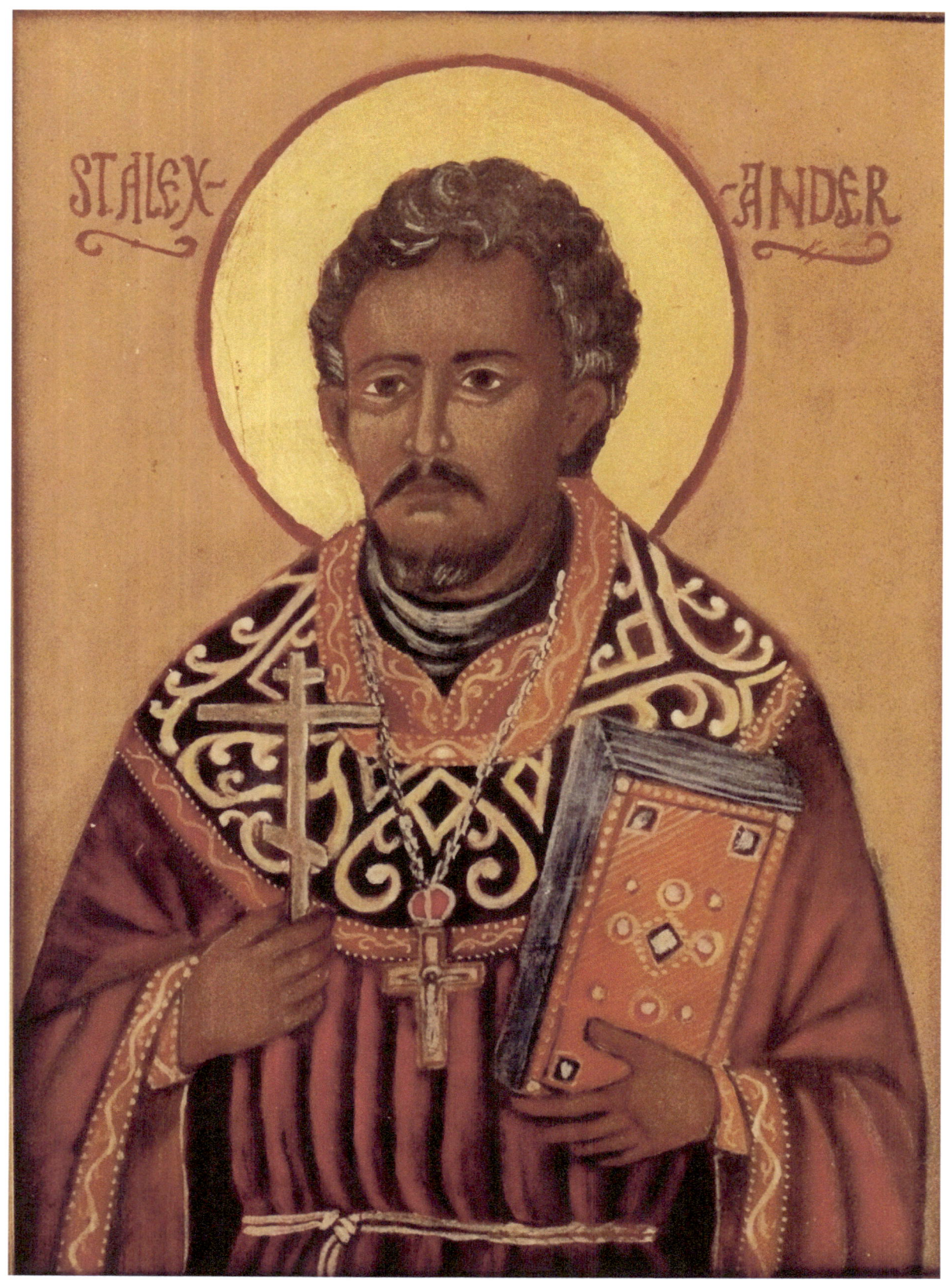

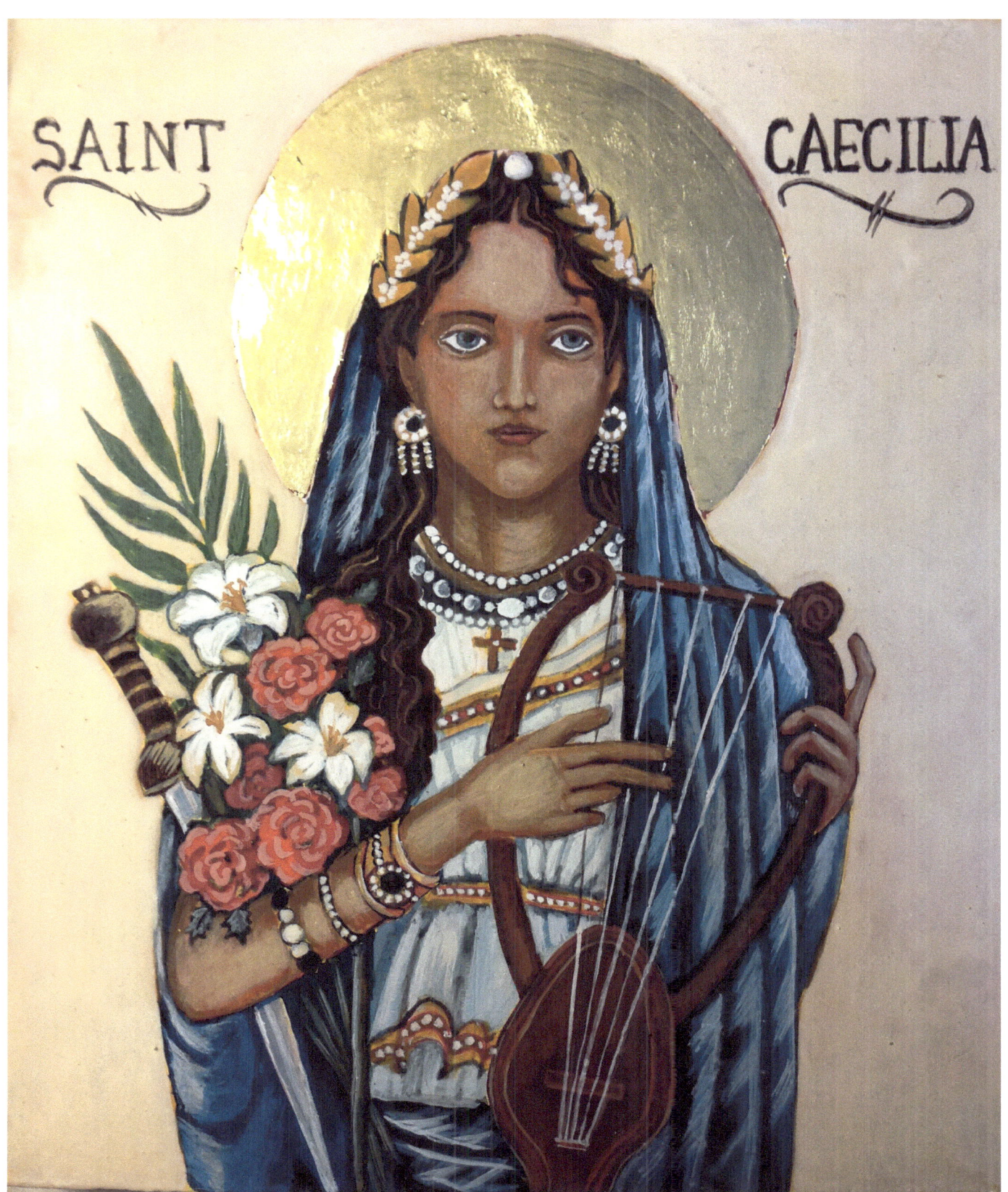

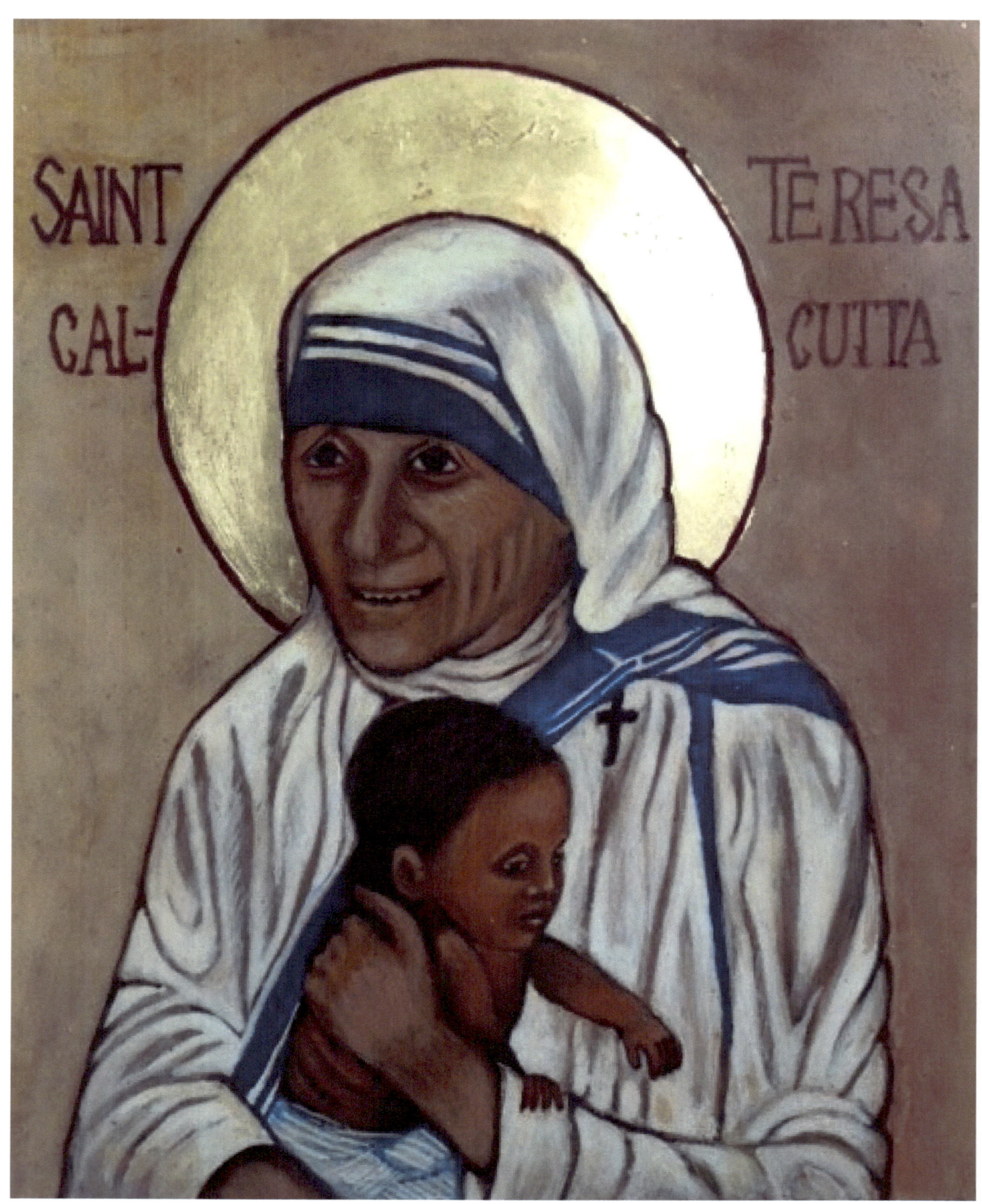

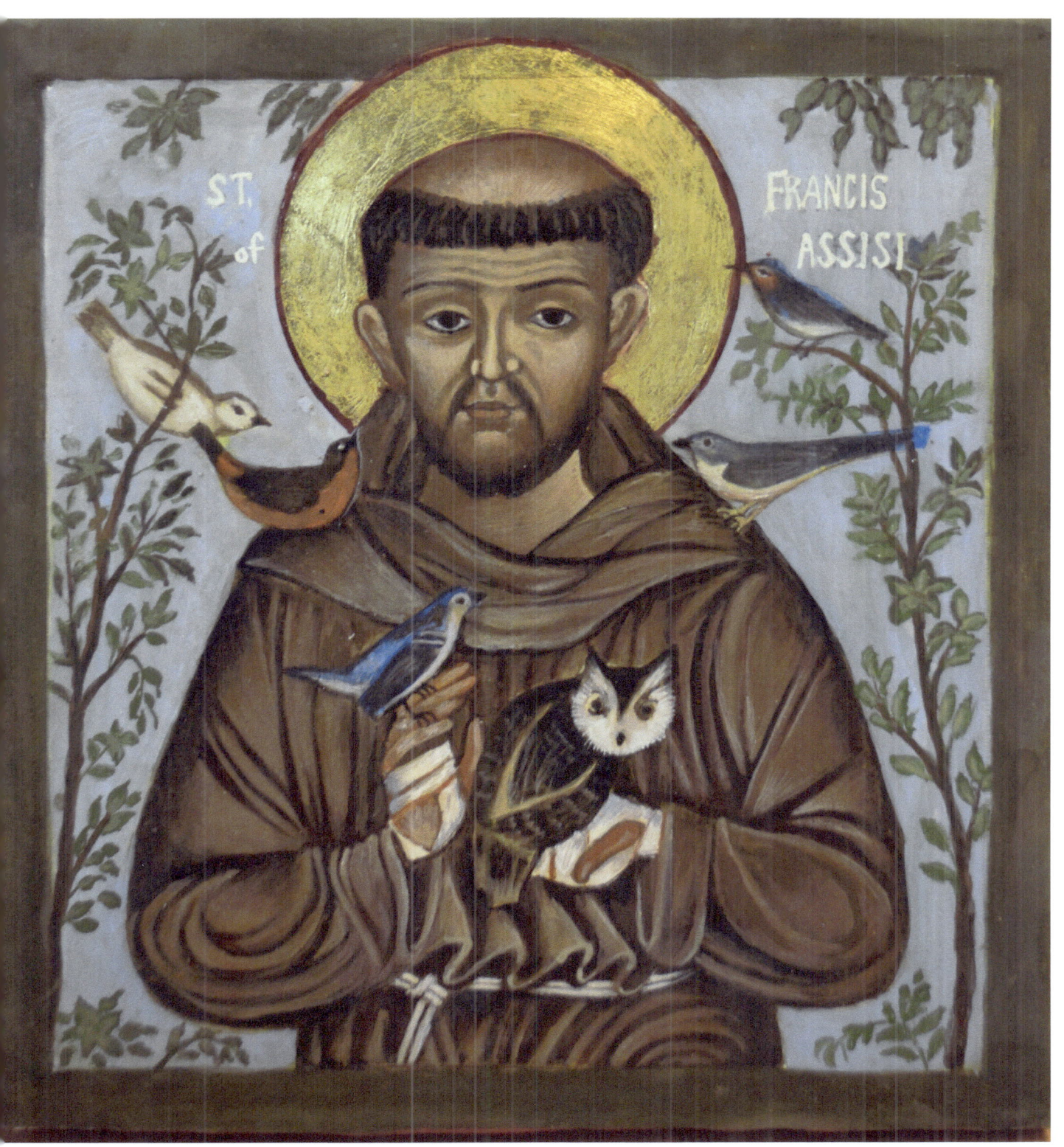

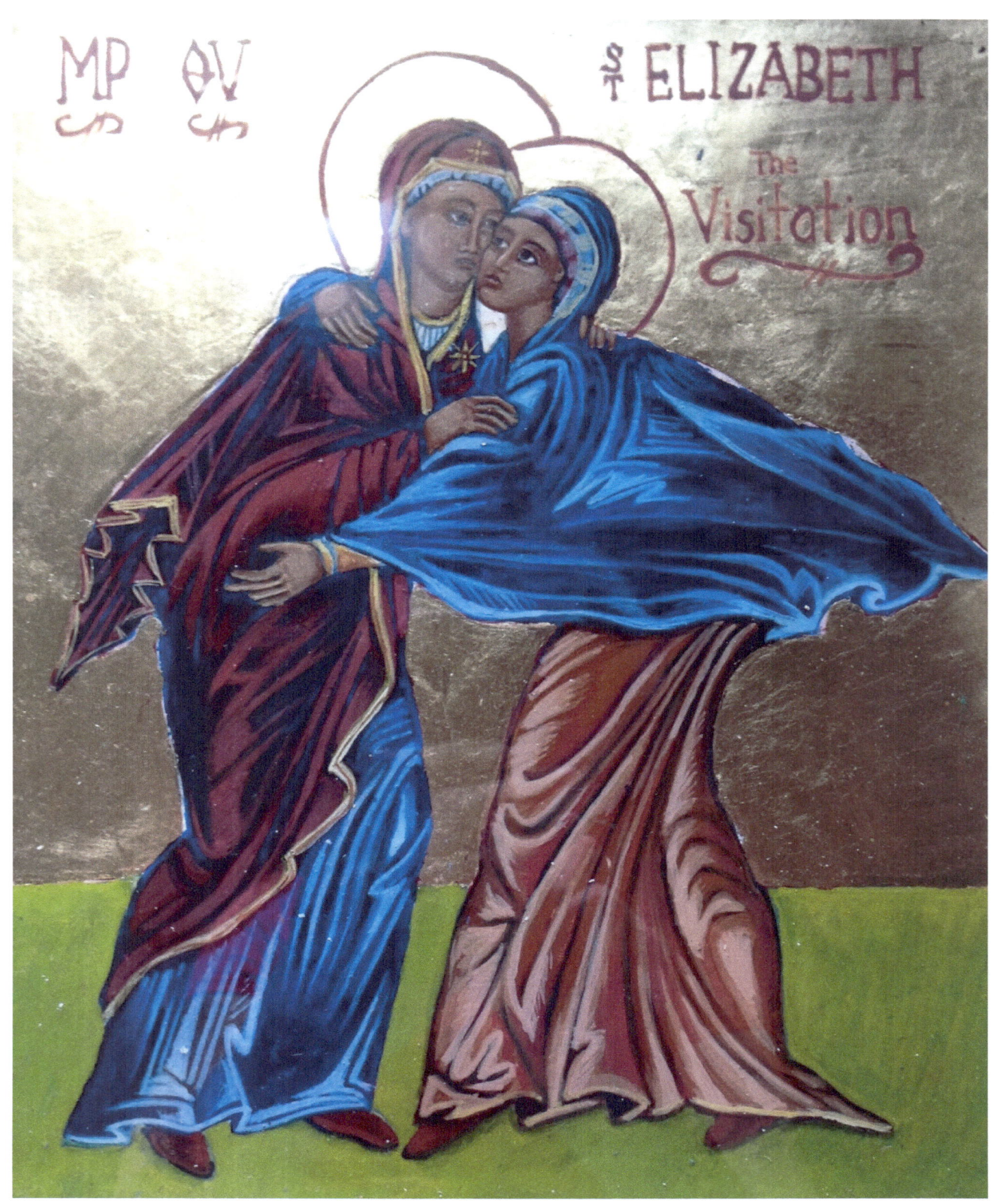

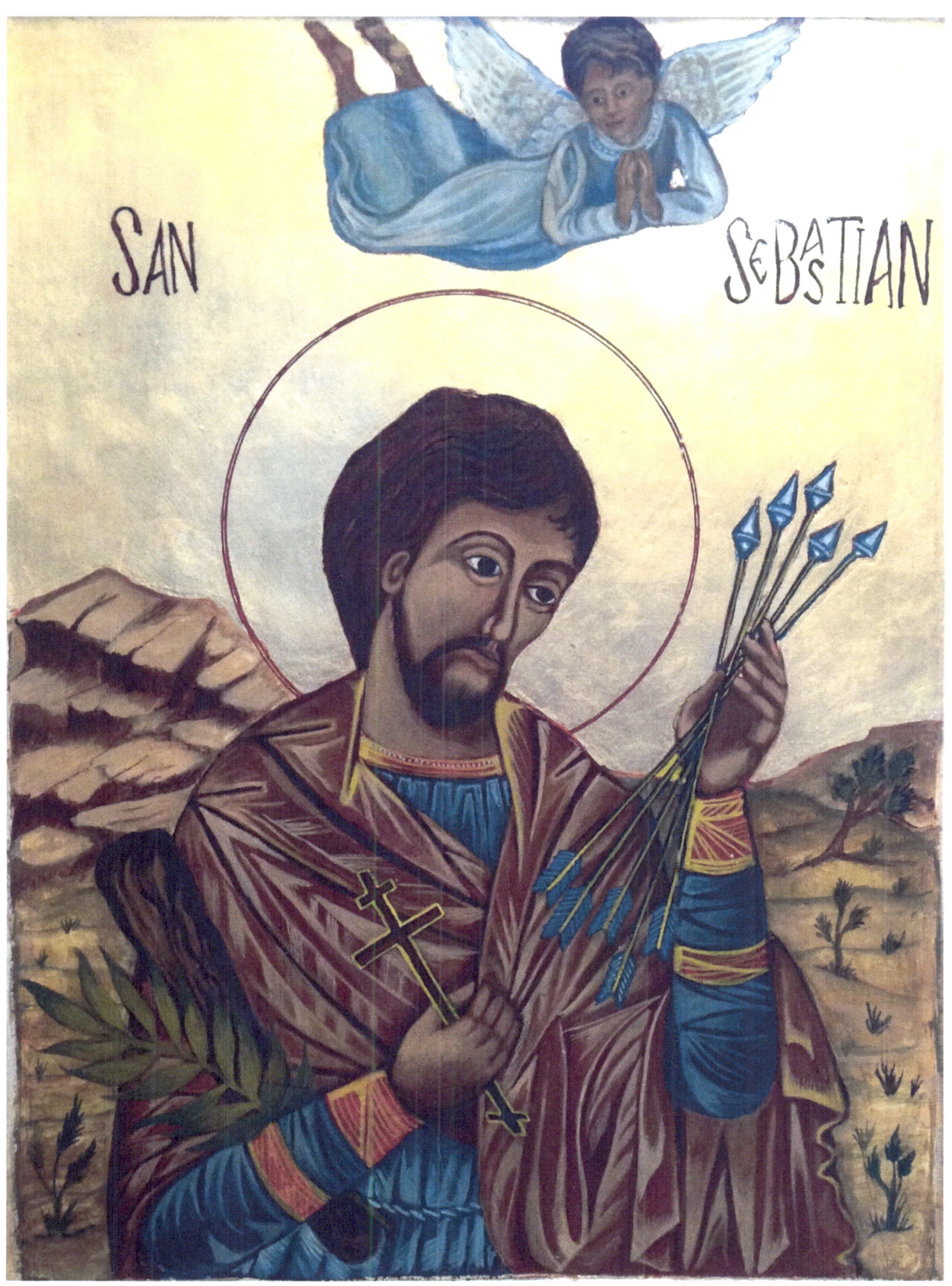

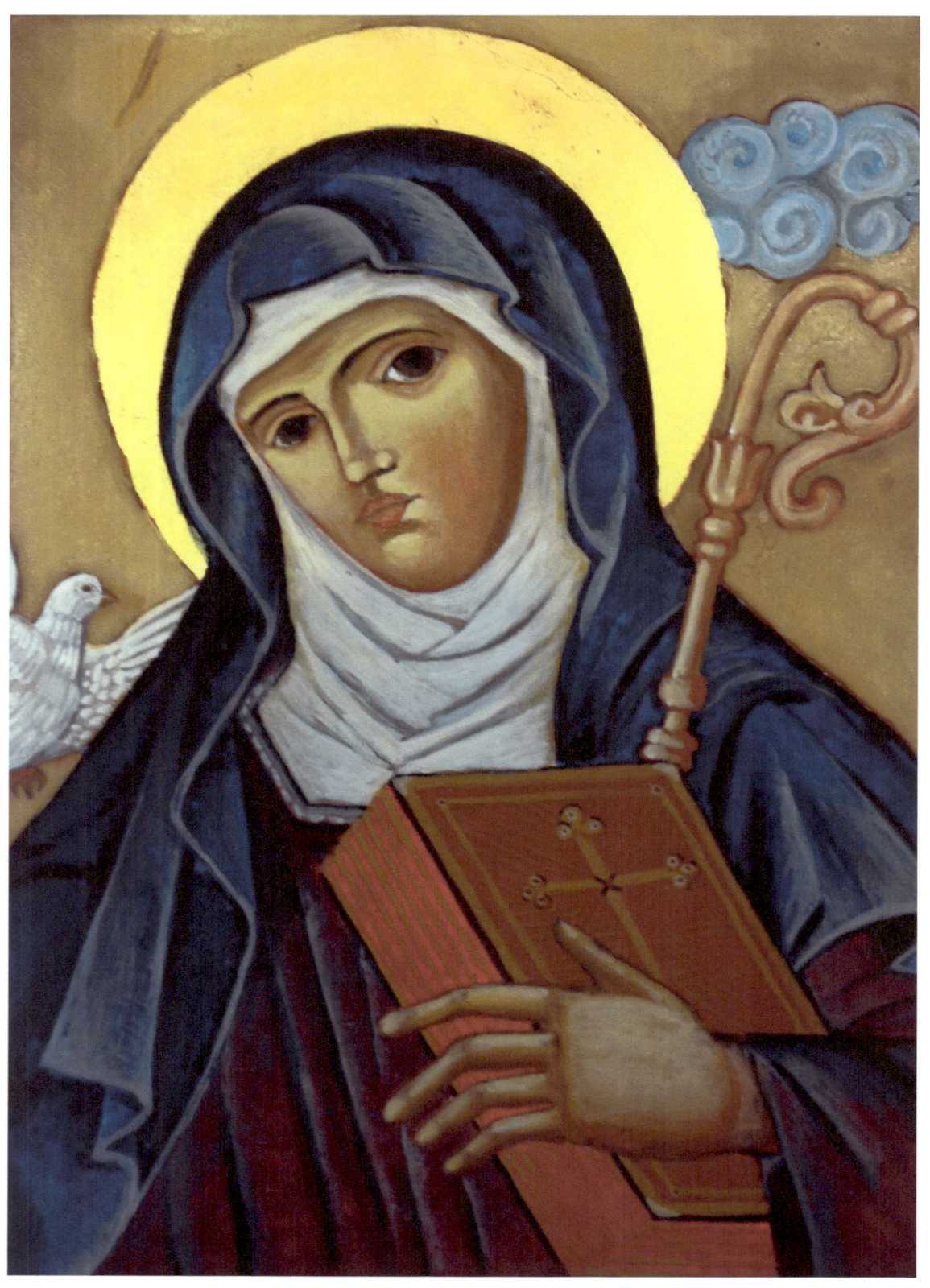

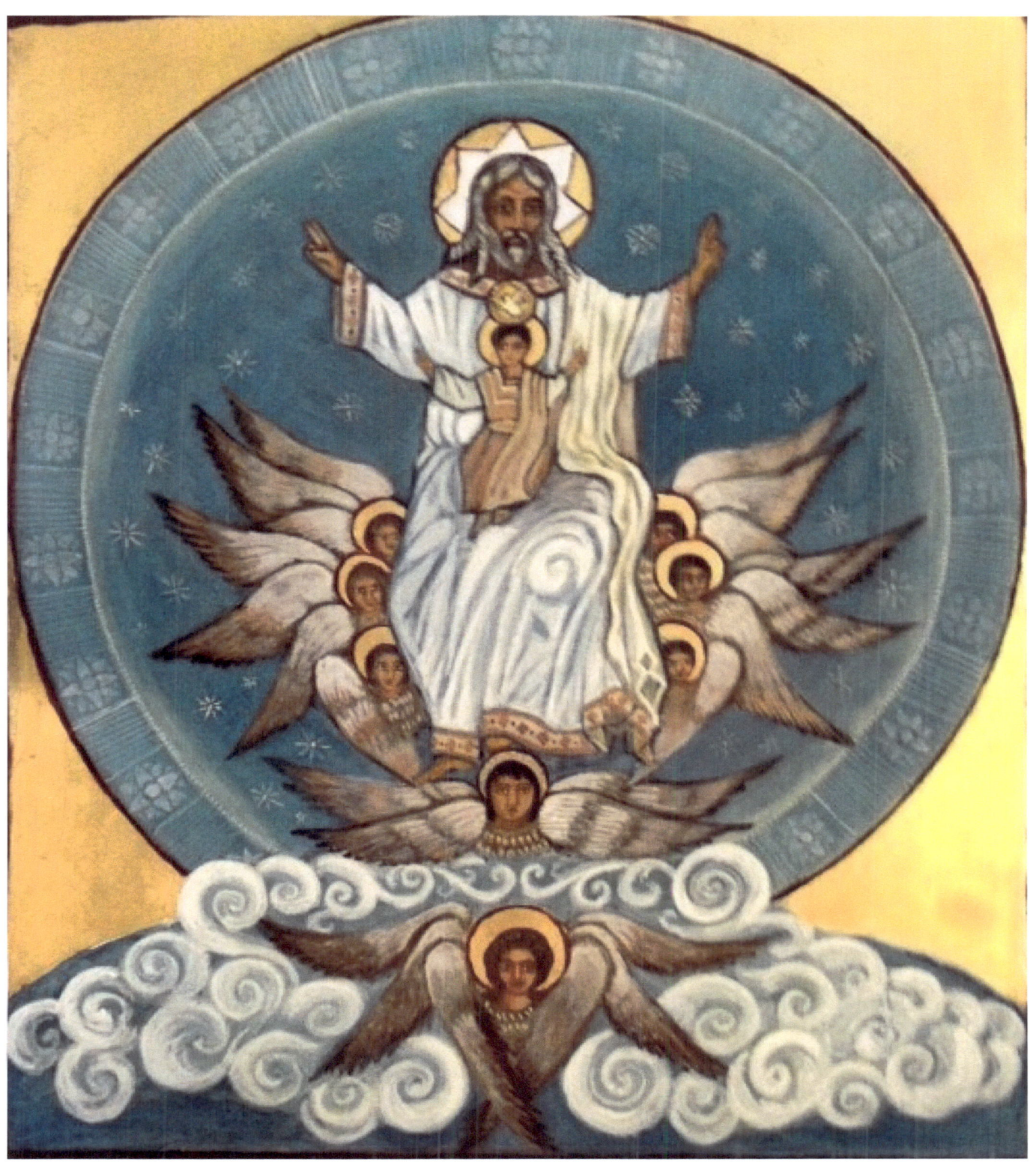

Icon Process

Each icon takes at least 30 hours of work. This includes preparing the board for the paint with 10 layers of gesso and sanding. Then, several coats of red clay where the gold is to be applied. All of that takes about Once the gold is laid, the painting begins. Paint is made with natural pigments mixed with egg yolk and water. The painting takes about 20 hours. Each face has at least 6 layers of progressively lighter colors applied.

Original Icon—prices

Original icon (9x11 approximate size, saint chosen by you)with one or two faces and minimal gold—$500.

Larger sizes, more gold leaf, or more faces—price goes up accordingly. Ask for an estimate.

Icon Prints—prices

Cards—$3 each

Canvas print—8x10 $50

Metal print—8x10—$60

Wood print—8x10—$75

Ask for estimates on different sized prints.

www.ingramcontent.com/pod-product-compliance
Lightning Source LLC
Chambersburg PA
CBHW041936240526
45473CB00034B/1748